Dec 16/12

You Were Born #1

By Syldia Bailey-Walker

Library of Congress Control Number:		2012907300
ISBN:	Hardcover	978-1-4691-2721-7
	Softcover	978-1-4691-2720-0
	Ebook	978-1-4691-2722-4

Author's e-mail address: *bornnumber1@rogers.com*

This book was printed in the United States of America.

To order additional copies of this book, contact:
Xlibris Corporation
1-888-795-4274
www.Xlibris.com
Orders@Xlibris.com
113245

Contents

To my mother, my father, my sisters, and my brothers, with my deepest love and affection

Praise for You Were Born #1

"If you read one self-help book cover to cover, let it be this one. I strongly recommend anyone looking for a life change to read *You Were Born #1.* Syldia sheds light on skills that are essential to success in not only your day-to-day life but also your career which is especially important in today's tough economy. She tackles tough subjects in a down to earth and relatable way. Highly recommended!"

—Stacee Samuels, B.Comm, CHRP
(Certified Human Resources Professional)

"As soon as I started to read I could feel Syldia's passion, enthusiasm and optimism. I think this is a great read for anyone who wants to live their life to the fullest, be inspired, happier, do more etc. Not many of us are able to naturally do this without a little reminder or nugget of golden advice. I feel inspired and encouraged".

—Denise Pitter, Actress and Singer

"Syldia is a person I look up to, an inspiration, a mentor in all aspects of life. Her ability to empower and inspire others is truly a gift to be shared. This book reflects her true passion and desire for one's success in life."

—Raya D,Instructor

"*You were Born #1* is an inspiring read. Given the pessimistic times many face in this day and age, this book really helps to motivate and encourage the hopeless and downtrodden. Emphasis on the difference a positive outlook makes on life can profoundly impact those who read it. I encourage anyone who is looking for a fresh perspective on life to read this book!"

—Keisha Carrington, Clinical Research Coordinator

Preface

For as long as I can remember, I have always felt like #1. Perhaps it was because of the way my parents raised my siblings and I that I am able to walk into any room with the poise and confidence of the most important person in that room, because of them, and because of the experiences that I have had throughout my life, I have never once forgotten that I am a special creation, put on this earth for a very important purpose.

In my opinion, it is up to each person to consider himself important; that is a truth that has never left me since it was instilled in me by my parents. Furthermore, the beauty and dynamism of the many strong, empowered women whom I have been blessed to call friends and relatives have affirmed my beliefs that people who are able to understand their own importance will waste a lot less time caught in the cycle of needing to please others and find much more joy in living a full and diverse life.

It has always been a dream of mine to write a book like this one to encourage those whose vision of their own importance is clouded by adversity and self-doubt. Sharing my vision of life with people who are facing affliction has allowed me to fine tune a gift I have always known I've had—the ability to sense the thoughts and feelings of others and meet their needs with advice and support. Through this book, I hope to communicate with you some of the truths that I have discovered while counseling and consoling others. I especially want to impart on you the truth that you—yes YOU—were born #1. You have the ability to do something very special with your life; you may just not be aware of how powerful you are.

The following chapters contain pieces of wisdom I have given many people on how to feel like #1 based on my own interests and personal habits. Because of my extremely diverse work experience and my interest in taking courses and seminars to enrich my skills and experience, I am able to offer insightful advice on a variety of topics, including fashion, social justice, personal administration, work habits, and parenting. My wish for you as you read this book is that you will find at least one nugget of encouragement to help you as you move along in your own journey towards a diverse and enriching life.

It's Up To You

Were you aware that your life began as an electrifying race? In a moment of passion, your father released you, along with a million other tiny spermatozoa, into a race toward life. Swimming up that stream of your mother's womb, you fought your way through the sea of sperm, pushing and darting past the others to meet the Egg—the warm cocoon that would be your new home if you made it to the finish line. Bang! With one last push, you left the flurry of the race behind you and sailed into the warm abyss of your mother's womb. As you entered your new home, you couldn't help feeling like a king in a castle.

"Wow!" you thought, "I am #1!"

As you cozied up to your new surroundings, there was no one to contest that you were the victor, the well-deserved first-place finisher of a difficult race.

Take a moment to reflect on that image of the spermatozoa at the finish line of the womb. Soak in the sense of victory; relish the feeling of well-deserved comfort. How often have you let those delightful feelings of being #1 sweep over you since the moment of conception? Do you live your life with the same sense of fearless passion you had when your life first began? If not, what is missing? Where did all your energy go?

From the moment you were conceived—in that do-or-die race to the finish line, you were armed with an astoundingly strong sense of self-will. It was self-will that made you push past the other sperm into your mother's womb. It was self-will that helped you grow from a tiny egg into a giggling baby, and it is self-will that will help you survive whatever comes next, no matter what stands in your way.

It's entirely up to an individual to choose to be #1. Just like that spermatozoa in the race to the womb, your self-will is what determines your victory. Far too many people suffer from low self-esteem and low expectations, but the truth is that no one can make you feel less than what you want yourself to be.

Something I have often heard people say is that they would have more self-esteem, "if only." I call this the "if only" clause.

"If only I was richer," they say.

Or "if only I was more popular."

Or "if only I looked better than I do now."

To this I say: rubbish! The secret to an unshakable self-esteem is the belief that empowerment is not limited to the rich, the famous, or the outwardly successful.

Let's examine the situation here: we were all created equally, we all came into the world the same way—naked and helpless, and unquestionably special. As life progressed, some of us may have stumbled upon a scrap of luck. We may have hit a jackpot or found fame somewhere along the line. Some of us may have achieved success with hard work, and some of us may still be pursuing success zealously.

Yet, all around, there are people who are still waiting for their fortune to fall their way, thinking, "When is it gonna be my turn?" If that sounds like you, I want to offer the following challenge: that you will begin to embrace the sense of self-will that you had when you were a tiny sperm swimming into your mother's womb and grab hold of the illustrious life that is rightfully yours. You were born with the right and the ability to succeed. You can achieve fortune and success if you are willing to dream big and work hard.

"But," you might say, "I don't have any strength of will left to take hold of the amazing life that is rightfully mine. So much has happened to me. I don't know how I can recover."

If something unfortunate has happened to you along your life's journey, don't let it maintain a hold on who you can be and what you can accomplish. Take the time now to learn to close the door on your past. Forgive and seek reconciliation. Deal with the situation and move on. Do whatever it takes to free yourself from the toxic waste of your past suffering so that, even in that, you can claim a personal victory.

As soon as you have freed yourself from the past, begin looking forward toward the future. Set for yourself a goal to aim for. Make a decision to get out of your discouragement and to look within yourself and think, "Right! I, and I alone, am responsible for my own happiness." Take responsibility for your own freedom and happiness in life and begin to create meaningful experiences for yourself. Believe in your ability to be successful. Fill yourself up with those feelings of being #1 by remembering the initial victory that brought you to life.

The beauty of birth is that it is the beginning of a victor's story. How the rest of that story plays out is up to you.

Don't Worry, Make Lemonade

Approximately twenty-two years ago, Bobby McFerrin snagged a #1 hit on Billboard's Hot 100 when he encouraged people everywhere to exchange the burden of constant worry for the buoyancy of happiness in his song "Don't Worry, Be Happy." Those four simple words were a call to quit complicating life by fretting over the inevitable and create happiness by smiling in the face of adversity.

It seems as if our society has an obsession with fretting over things we cannot control. After all, if anyone has a doubt about how deeply this problem has taken root in our society, they can check the Billboard charts. Songs like "Don't Worry, Be Happy" succeed because they remind people of their need to free themselves from the prisons of worry and stress that trap them on a day-to-day basis.

What is it about the practice of worrying that makes it such a hard habit to break? We all know that a build-up of worries quickly leads to stress. Scientific literature has proven to us that stress is the #1 cause of illnesses and chronic health concerns such as high blood pressure, diabetes, and heart failure. Yet somehow, many of us can't seem to stop ourselves from becoming overwhelmed by our worries.

It is not wrong to have concerns. We need to be concerned about our surroundings, our neighbourhood, our families, our jobs, our finances, and our health in order to lead happy lives. However, it is when we allow our concerns to turn into worries that they become detrimental to our lives. So, how can we prevent our concerns from turning into worries? We do it by being conscious of the attitude we have when we are presented with a dilemma.

Let's say for example, that you heard a rumour in the break room one day that your company is planning to downsize. Before the rumour has a chance to become reality, you begin to worry. You begin to have sleepless nights, you stop taking vacation days as a way to increase your productivity and impress your boss, and you start cutting your personal budget because you fear you may not have a job the following year. Slowly but surely, this unfounded sense of fear begins to have control over every choice you make and every attitude you have until you find yourself drowning in feelings of helplessness and victimization.

What is wrong with this scenario? Is your concern about potentially not having a job illegitimate? Were you overcompensating in your decision to stop taking vacation days so you could increase your productivity? Should you have acted like you hadn't heard the rumour at all and take no precautions? No! In fact, the decisions you made to work harder, to become more valuable to the company, and to adjust your personal budget were very wise. What was problematic was the attitude that fueled your new behaviour: fear.

The world has developed many interesting methods of coping with fear: false bravado, worry-driven hard work, escaping from fear through procrastination, substance abuse, the media, etc. The characteristic all of these coping mechanisms share is their penchant for bottling up disruption, devastation, and confusion and preventing any emotional healing from taking place. What, then, is the solution to the very natural feeling of fear that rises in every human begin in the face of uncertainty? I would like to suggest a rather controversial remedy I believe to be truly effective in combating fear when examined in the larger scheme of the cosmos: faith.

Take a look, if you will, at all the different species on earth and examine how they deal with worry. Examine birds, for example. Do they appear to be worried about anything? They are always moving, flying from place to place, singing and chirping wherever they go. When they build their nests, do they worry about something coming and destroying that nest? Perhaps. But, when something does come along and destroy their nest—accidents, bad weather, or the interference of mankind, they simply move onto another location and begin to work on building another, singing and chirping as they did while they were creating their first home.

Birds—like most other living species on our planet—possess a faith that most humans can only dream of having. They live with a peaceful sense of certainty that they will be taken care of. Even though most living things cannot acknowledge the greater source of their provision, they believe in its existence and their ability to remain resilient in the face of difficult circumstances stems from that great sense of faith that they have.

So then, let's go back to the scenario I mentioned earlier about a company downsizing their work force. What can we do, as human beings in that kind of situation, to develop the resilience to push through? My suggestion is that we combat each realistic fear with faith in the possibility of a better tomorrow. Take a moment to stop and reflect after that rumour filters into your ears in the break room. Ask yourself: is losing my job really an inevitable part of my future, or am I just predicting an unhappy ending for myself to protect myself from feelings of disappointment? Each time your head hits the pillow, combat the fearful thoughts swirling through your head with a proverb that reminds you that tomorrow is a new day full of unwritten opportunities. When you find yourself buried waist-deep in work that you have taken on to impress your boss, make a plan to balance out your workload so that high-stress situations don't have the opportunity to leave you feeling paralyzed before your boss even sees what a good job you have done.

Making choices in faith that tomorrow holds the possibility for better returns will help you to make wiser choices—choices that will ultimately benefit you, whether life gives you the cake you deserve or the lemons you weren't expecting.

So what happens if life does give you lemons you weren't expecting? In the scenario of the company downsizing, what should you do if you happen to be one of the employees that gets laid off? My suggestion is this: if your company has decided to downsize and you are part of the group that gets cut, be thankful for the experience, the salary, and the opportunities for professional development you have had over the years and move on. Instead of moaning, worrying, and causing yourself to be sick, choose to see your job loss as an opportunity for a better, albeit different, tomorrow. Remember, every person has the potential to be successful if he puts his mind and energy into whatever he does. The decision is up to him and him alone.

As you move forward, holding life's lemons in your hand, take the time to learn how to be creative. Take the sour experience of losing a job and create a new opportunity for personal growth. It may be the change that you needed in your life to propel you into the new avenues that can unleash your hidden potential.

Finally, remember that happiness is not something you can purchase with money, earn with talent, or find in the world's vast opportunities for temporary escape. It is a choice you make, regardless of the situation you are in, to move forward with a positive attitude. I can assure you that, with a commitment to staying positive in your mind, faith in a better tomorrow in your heart, and a bright smile on your face, you will find you have the perfect dose of sugar you need to take life's lemons and make lemonade.

Attire

It's not just the

clothes and make-up,

it's the *attitude*.

First Impressions Count

Many people underestimate the long lasting impact of a first impression. When the first impression someone receives from you is negative, it will significantly hinder their ability to trust you and thus, will affect your working relationship with them from the very start.

On the other hand, a positive first impression will go a long way in helping you build rapport and thus, will set you on the path to reaping the benefits of a good relationship.

With this in mind, it is important to note that proper attire, careful grooming and good hygiene are essential to giving people the impression that you truly are the #1 person you were born to be.

Morning bedhead is never appropriate for any kind of public event. Make sure you comb your hair before leaving the house and keep a comb with you to tend to flyaways and stay neat on windy days.

Keeping your hands in your pocket signals to the people around you that you are apathetic. This type of attitude is undesirable in any kind of professional setting and the appearance of it should be avoided at all costs.

Any untucked shirt is a symbol of sloppiness. Take great care to ensure that your apparel is always fitted and worn properly.

Work clothes should be properly washed and ironed so that they are free of wrinkles. Wrinkled clothing communicates laziness and disorganization.

Sloppy Joe

Slouching conveys a lack of confidence. On the other hand, practicing good posture can be beneficial for both your spine and your self-esteem.

Scuffed shoes and untied shoelaces communicate heedlessness. Double knot your shoelaces to keep them from always coming loose.

Confident eye-contact can help you come across as intelligent and positively assertive.

A well-fitted jacket that has been ironed gives you a professional look that is both sharp and fresh.

Clean and Polished

Standing with your hands casually resting at your sides communicates respect and makes you seem approachable and friendly.

Wearing a belt can help you prevent your pants from slipping. It can also help to provide the traction you need to keep your shirt-tails tucked in.

Properly fitted pants should rest just below the ankles and drape neatly across the tops of your shoes.

Make sure your shoes are clean and well-polished. Men's footwear may not be as flashy as women's footwear, but clean shoes, however simple, will communicate a lot about proper hygiene and personal care.

Workplace Attire

Many women subscribe to the faulty belief that they must dress like men in order to gain respect in the office.

Unfortunately, this misconception leads them to limit their workplace attire to power suits and menswear-inspired outfits that, more often than not, overwhelm their naturally graceful figures and do nothing to accentuate their unique personalities.

As a woman, you can bring a distinct set of qualities along with you into the workplace. Naturally feminine qualities such as tenderness, warmth, elegance and poise inspire a kind of positive dynamic in any workplace that is difficult to resist.

Allow these beautiful, womanly qualities to shine by acknowledging your femininity through your professional wardrobe.

A pressed, white blouse buttoned-up all the way will make you seem severe and uptight.

A structured blazer can overwhelm a tiny figure, especially if it is not the right fit.

Although shoulder pads are designed to help a garment hang nicely on a person's frame, this design feature may contribute to emphasizing poor fit of the blazer.

When attempting to be assertive, opt for a confident stance (with the chest slightly pushed out and shoulders rolled back), rather than crossed arms because crossing your arms communicates that you are either unapproachable or apathetic.

Frumpy loafers may seem more functional, but they lack the tasteful formality that is desirable in an office setting.

Another faux-pas is wearing athletic shoes with a business or formal outfit. If driving or travelling to work in your work shoes is uncomfortable for you, leave a few pairs of work shoes at the office so that you can change into them when you arrive at the office.

It's Not A Man's World

Be wary of central air conditioning at office complexes! Wear an extra layer underneath your outfit if you are cold to prevent slouching.

Dress pants should sit comfortably on the hips and drape straight down without bunching.

Bunching usually means that the pant does not fit properly or the pant is not structured enough for work attire.

Instead of the traditional boxy blazer, try one that is made for the female figure. Look for darts and princess seams on the garment that helps fit your curves better.

Even small details will help your outfit to look less like a uniform. Try a shawl lapel or garments with embellished cuffs.

Collect accessories that add a hint of femininity to any outfit, such as a belt with a bow or a floral pin.

Wearing heels – even if they are low in height will encourage you to stand in a more ladylike posture, which will contribute to a poised appearance.

An added bonus is that heels give the illusion of more toned calves and longer legs!

Elegant and Empowered

Take an extra five minutes in the morning to style your hair so that you can leave it down. Allowing your hair to frame your face will soften your look and draw people's attention towards your radiant smile.

Soften the harsh feel of a blazer or structured blouse by pairing it with a flirty pencil skirt.

The tapered bottom of the pencil skirt gives off a professional feel, while the natural curvature of the style accentuates your womanly figure.

For those with a pear-shaped body, an A-line skirt will help balance out those curvaceous hips.

Colour blocking by wearing different colours on the top and bottom will help you avoid creating a boxy silhouette.

FUN WITH TEXTURE

You can play with contrast by pairing lighter fabrics, such as silk and chiffon, with more structured fabrics like wool or tweed.

Stripes and Fit

Many women make the mistake of buying clothes that are not suitable for their body type, in an effort to stay on top of the trends. Unfortunately, wearing clothes that don't fit properly counteracts any effort a person makes to be stylish or fashionable.

To avoid this problem, remember that the right outfit should accentuate your best features and downplay the weaker parts of your figure. A good rule of thumb to follow when choosing whether or not to follow a trend is this: if it doesn't fit right, don't try to make it work.

Voluminous hairstyles can sometimes cause your face to look broader than it actually is. Stick to a sleek hairstyle that keeps the hair out of your face. Add visual interest by using accessories or by adding subtle styling details like loose curls or braids.

Crew neck tops that cover the décolletage draw unnecessary attention to a fuller chest and negatively highlight a rounded figure.

While horizontal stripes continue to be a recurring trend, the width and direction of stripes should be considered when purchasing a striped garment.

Horizontal stripes lead the eye to travel across the body. This creates the illusion of a wider frame.

Thinner stripes or stripes in a chevron pattern are more flattering options for curvier figures.

Straight-cut skirts emphasize the width of full hips and dresses that extend past the knee make you appear shorter than you actually are.

To look taller, choose garments that make your legs look longer and minimize your torso.

The Weight of Stripes

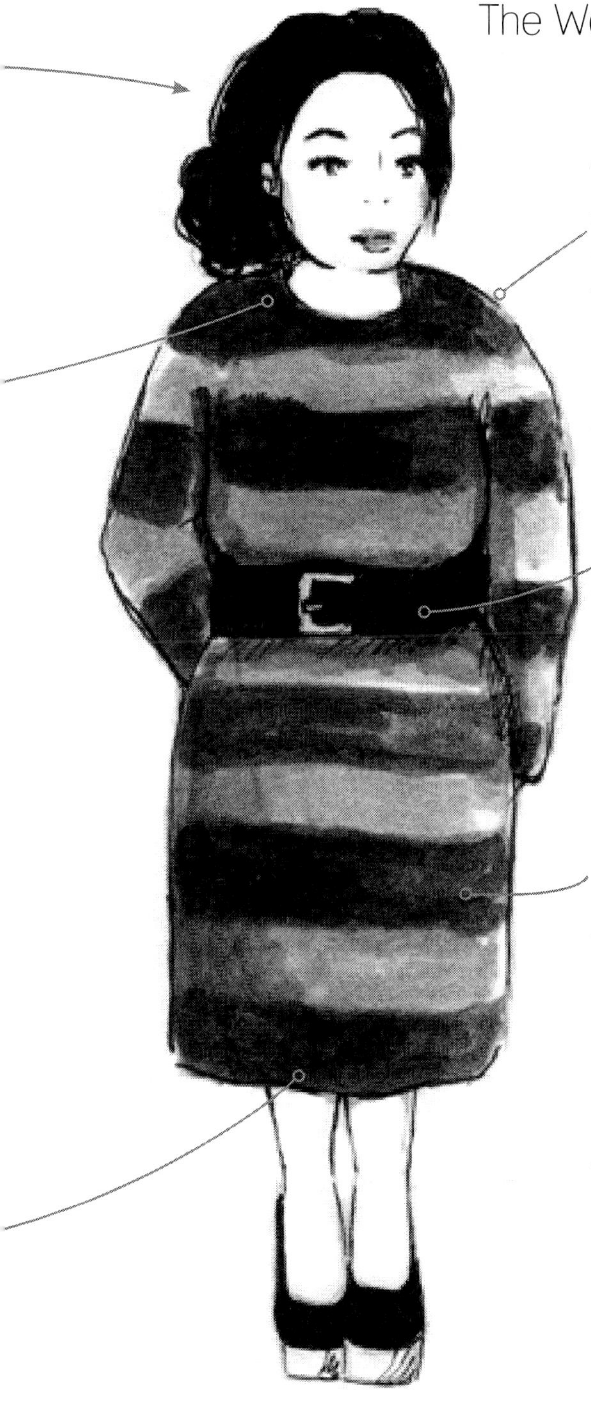

Thick fabrics such as wool and tweed add the illusion of weight to the body and should be worn sparingly.

Thick belts can emphasize a wide mid-section instead of creating a smaller waistline like a thinner belt would.

Pull-over dresses that have no structure tailored into them make the body look columnar, thereby giving you a very unflattering silhouette. This is also the case with body-clinging fabrics such as jersey cotton or static-prone materials, such as polyester or rayon.

Embrace Your Curves the Right Way.

A deep-V or scoop neckline causes the eye to look vertically rather than horizontally.

The lower neckline highlights your décolletage and creates the illusion of a longer, narrower face.

Accordion pleats and vertical stripes draw the eye downward, thereby downplaying your body's width and giving the illusion of height.

Despite the lengthening effect that vertical stripes have, wide stripes can still create the unflattering effect of unwanted curves.

Choose an empire-waisted dress or create one by cinching the upper part of your waist – right under your chest area – with a thin belt. Empire-waisted dresses give the illusion of height.

Since the area right under your bust is the thinnest part of your torso area, it also conveniently hides problematic tummy areas.

When shopping for skirts and dresses, opt for a loose sheath-cut or structured A-line style.

Sheath-cut skirts in a looser fabric highlight fuller hips but allow enough room to camouflage wider thighs.

Structured A-line skirts are flattering to almost all body types because they draw the attention away from the hips towards the hemline..

Knee-length skirts help you appear modest while still giving you a chance to show off your great calves!

Where your hem line stops is usually where your eye is drawn to. This is important to know if you want to accentuate the thinner parts of your legs (at the ankle and right at the knee) and draw attention away from thicker areas of your body, such as the widest part of your calves and thighs.

Mix and Match

How you choose to dress every day is a great way to showcase the various elements of your personality. However, the feeling that everything in an outfit needs to match often stops people from translating their personal idiosyncrasies into their attire.

The truth is: simply matching everything has long gone out of style! Instead, the art of mixing and matching interesting and complementary pieces has become the contemporary trend. Learning the art of mix and match will not only add spice to your wardrobe, it will also extend the wearability of each piece of clothing or jewelry you own, because you can now wear them in more ways than one!

Hiding your face under stingy bangs makes you look sickly, tired and gaunt.

Don't waste the opportunity to add interest to your outfit by layering a flashier top under a more demure jacket.

Also, wear your jacket open or with the sleeves rolled up so that a secondary top layer or fun jewelry pieces can peek out.

A boxier top should always be paired with a more slim fitting bottom. Wearing a broad-shouldered jacket with a bootcut jean will make you look columnar and will add unnecessary width to your silhouette.

Try to avoid falling into the trap of picking an outfit in a monochromatic colour scheme when creating an outfit. Monochromatic outfits can be unpleasantly matchy and too much denim can make you look washed-out.

Again, the key here is to use contrast to create a dynamic and memorable outfit. You can do this by varying colour and mixing fabrics with different weights and textures.

FEELING ADVENTUROUS?

Try mixing leather with lace!

Wear a tight fitted leather jacket over a soft lace dress to create a beautiful balance between the loud leather and the feminine touch of lace peeking out under it

Drive Away the Dull

Denim jeans should never be paired with a denim top without an accessory in an accent colour to break up the monotony.

Pair a full-denim outfit with a bright white tee shirt or a colourful scarf for a more interesting look.

Make sure your jeans are not so long that they drag on the ground as you walk. Pants that are too long are a safety hazard and bedraggled cuffs create an undesirable sloppy look.

High Contrast Flair.

Use accessories such as long necklaces and bangles to add some bohemian flair.

Your purse doesn't always have to be the same colour as your outfit or shoes! Choose a clutch or bag in a complementary colour or neutral metallic to introduce some variation.

This bold choice will provide as a focal point and add a little something special to the outfit!

Keeping your bangs out of your face will go a long way in making you look and feel refreshed.

Pair a denim vest with a flowy dress to create an interesting contrast of stiff and loose fabrics.

The softer fabric adds a more feminine touch to the outfit and balances out the masculine feel of the denim vest.

A maxi dress in a gentle A-line can give the illusion of height if it fits properly.

This dress is perfect to wear by itself, as it demonstrates the Single Erogenous zone rule. Since your legs are covered up, your arms are free to be accessorized with loud bangles and bracelets!

Avoid looking costume-y by skipping the most obvious choice to pair denim with a pair of cowboy boots from your closet. Fashion is all about the unexpected! Pair coarse denim with a more traditional pair of Mary-Janes or ballet flats in a bold colour to add an element of surprise to the bottom of your outfit.

Dressing Up

A semi-formal event is the perfect time to pull out that outfit you've left tucked away in your closet because it gives off too much pizazz for an ordinary day. However, while getting dolled up may be fun, it is good to be cautious that you don't go overboard with accessories and trim.

When picking an outfit for a dressier occasion, remember that elegance and sophistication are usually synonymous with simplicity. Allow yourself the freedom to add a bit of sparkle to your semi-formal attire but be careful not to douse yourself in it!

Chandelier earrings and other types of statement jewelry should be paired with simpler outfits. Otherwise, they have an overpowering effect.

The key here is to choose a focal point and stick with it. It might be tempting to layer everything on -- from your grandma's pearls to your vintage one of a kind dress, but, by doing this, no single item seems special anymore, because they are all trying to outshine one another. By concentrating on either your dress or your accessories, people will be able to spot the one thing you most want highlighted.

A decorative detail should not overpower the overall look of the dress. You want people to remember how beautiful you looked in the dress, not how big the bow on you was.

Always check the invitation to make sure you are dressed for the right occasion.

A full-length gown is most appropriate for gala events or black-tie weddings. Opt for a cocktail dress or tea-length dress when attending semi-formal events.

If in doubt, check with the host of the event to confirm the appropriate dress code for the evening.

Drowning in Details

Tiaras are best saved for occasions when you are the guest of honour, e.g. your birthday or your wedding day.

LAST CHECK:

Make sure to check no under-garments are showing!

Look for too-sheer fabrics or bra straps falling out of place.

If you want your dress to be the centre of attention, save chandelier earrings for a dress with fewer built-in accents. Choose a pair of rhinestone studs or simple pearl earrings instead.

A little bit of trim can go a long way. Opt for subtle ruffles in the bust area to add volume to a smaller chest or choose a dress with a sash to create the illusion of a cinched waist.

Stay demure by choosing a dress that is slightly above the knee or longer for a more formal event.

T-strap heels elongate wide feet and give the illusion of narrowness.

Sleek and Stylish

When wearing a dress with trim, it is best to opt for a simple jewelry such as a pearl necklace or pendant and chain.

A shiny clutch can add a lot more pizazz to a more plain-looking dress. Allow accessorics like your purse and shoes to dress up your outfit for you sometimes, instead of always choosing to wear a dress that is heavily ornamented or over-designed.

COLOUR CODED

Dark neutrals such as black, navy, charcoal, and brown communicate sophistication and flatter the figure.

Dresses made of darker colours create the illusion of a smaller body because they reflect less light than dresses made of light-coloured material. In addition, fabrics such as velvet absorb light and create an interesting sheen as light ripples through the texture of the fabric without all the sparkle.

Deep jewel tones such as emerald, royal blue, teal, and violet are good examples of brighter colours that can help you express your fun side while maintaining your air of elegance.

If you choose to wear a brighter dress, pair it with neutral or subdued accessories to create a sense of balance.

Date Night

When dressing up for date night, it can be tempting to flaunt every feature of your body in an attempt to be sexy. Unfortunately, showing too much skin can often have an adverse effect because it leaves nothing to the imagination.

A good rule to remember when dressing for a hot date is this: less is more. Contrary to popular opinion, true sexiness is not the lack of lady-like modest; instead, it is the perfect balance of mystery and revelation that leaves the onlooker wanting more.

Too much hair product can leave your tresses looking like a mangy bird's nest. On date night, this may deter your date from engaging in any simple forms of affection –like tucking your hair behind your ear – because they are afraid to get their hand tangled amongst your sticky locks!

Remember that the way you carry yourself communicates a lot about your intelligence and self-worth. Make sure you always maintain an air of lady-likeness about you if you want to be treated like a lady.

Choosing to show both excessive cleavage and a lot of leg gives onlookers a negative impression of your sexual prowess.

The rule here is to choose that people in the fashion industry call the "Single Erogenous Zone" rule and only emphasize one bodily feature. If your skirt is a tad on the short side, try pairing it with a top that has a higher neckline.

WEARING SOMETHING SHORT?

When wearing a dress that shows a lot of leg, be very conscious of how you stand and sit. Standing with your legs together and sitting with your legs crossed or tucked to the side can help you avoid the kind of wardrobe malfunctions that could potentially tarnish your reputation.

Sensual Overdose

A skin-tight dress leaves little to the imagination and will only draw towards you the undesirable attention of predators.

When going out, choose only one piece of statement jewelry. In this case, opt for either the hoop earrings or the anklet, not both.

A hand on the hip communicates confidence and independence, while closed legs help retain an air of sophistication and poise.

Pack light. The point of going on a date is to have fun and hopefully get to know someone better. A large purse often alludes to a sense of high-maintenance and will also cause some discomfort to your back because of its weight.

A Touch of Mystery

When the dress you choose to wear is rather plain, you can add a bit of spice to your look by applying more dramatic make-up. Try a bold shade of eyeshadow or add a little hint of glitter – just make sure not to go overboard.

A simple way to start your make-up is to select a key feature on your face to emphasize. If you are going to mesmerize your date with your smoldering smoky-eye, leave the bold, red lipstick for the second date. Too much make-up will make you look overly dramatic and clown-like.

When choosing an outfit for a night out, select one part of the body you want to highlight and cover up the rest.

In this case, since the dress shows a lot of leg, the chest and arms are covered up to maintain the adequate amount of mystery needed to exude true sexiness.

IF THE SHOE FITS...

Remember to choose the right outfit for the right activity. While heels will accentuate the length of your legs, wearing them to a sports outing will make you look uncomfortably out of place.

Don't know what you'll be doing? Invest in a pair of light, foldable flats that can fit in your purse so that you will be prepared for any romantic activity – including long walks on the beach and a night full of dancing!

Procrastination

Unsuccessful people often blame external circumstances for keeping them from achieving their goals. I've heard people say in resignation: "The odds are stacked against me" or "It's just too hard!" I have come to the realization that the majority of complaints people have about why they are not able to complete a task are actually excuses they use to cover up the all-too-common and ultimately crippling habit of procrastination.

The most typical excuse that people give for why they procrastinate is lack of motivation.

"But I just don't feel like doing it!" some might say.

"I'm waiting for something to inspire me to do the work," others will add.

The ugly truth is that no one or nothing will ever inspire you to step out of the rut of procrastination for long. In chapter one, I mentioned the key to reclaiming personal victory in every area of your life is to strengthen your own willpower. Like the spermatozoa swimming toward the egg, you are engaged in a winner-take-all race to find and achieve your life's unique purpose. Procrastination is your willpower's arch-nemesis. Think of what happens to any spermatozoa that waits even a second before setting off on that initial race. You can be absolutely sure that he will not be the first one to arrive at the finish line. In life, just as in a race, every second counts.

"So what do I do if I am feeling unmotivated?" you might ask me. To this dilemma, I offer three pieces of advice.

First, remind yourself that external motivation is essentially a myth. If you are waiting for some sort of external force to descend upon you and drive you into action, you will never accomplish anything because that force is not going to come. You alone have the tools to start the fire of passion within you that will make your work meaningful.

Second, convince yourself to get started on a project even if you don't "feel" like doing it at the time. Trick yourself into doing something by telling yourself, "I'll just throw myself into this activity for five minutes. If I still feel completely unmotivated, then maybe I will switch to something else." I guarantee you that if you make those five minutes count, you will, more often than not, see your project to completion.

Third, see your life in terms of "small victories." Our brains are wired with a chemical called dopamine that rewards us with happy feelings every time we accomplish something. By breaking down our tasks into smaller sub-tasks and rewarding ourselves with a small treat after accomplishing a sub-task or two, we are likely to want to continue doing what we are doing because our dopamine system will kick in and remind us how good it felt to check off completed tasks on our to-do list.

That being said, I believe that lack of motivation is actually a superficial diagnosis of why people actually procrastinate. In my opinion, the three real reasons people procrastinate are the following: 1) the fear of failure, 2) the fear of success, and 3) the collection of mainly self-centered goals. Let me address each of these one at a time.

The fear of failure

The fear of failure is one of the most commonly undiagnosed reasons people procrastinate. When you hear someone say "this is too hard" or "the odds are stacked against me," they are actually admitting that they are afraid of not being able to meet the standard they (or most often, society) have set as a goal. Procrastination, then, is an outflow of their mental and emotional paralysis; fear has them believing they will be humiliated for trying and failing and thus they refuse to try at all.

How do you combat the fear of failure? Remind yourself that success and failure are relative terms. Refuse to allow society to define "success" and "failure" for you. Set achievable goals and work towards them, rewarding yourself for small victories, as I mentioned earlier. Remind yourself that you were born #1! You've already won the race that brought you to life. Anything you do now should be inspired by the glory of that victory. This concept of not resting on your laurels leads well into the next reason people procrastinate: the fear of success.

The fear of success

I never understood the very popular notion that you should "quit while you're ahead," yet so many people nowadays live by that philosophy. After all, shouldn't success inspire more success? Why would someone who has achieved a personal victory be content with mediocrity? Allow me to provide an example of what I mean.

Every so often, when a management position in a company opens up, there is talk in the break room about which employees would be the top contenders for receiving the forthcoming promotion. Most of the time, these sorts of predictions are made based on previous work performance and the top contenders are usually people who have shown great diligence or strong leadership capabilities. When the names of these individuals are brought up in conversation and the people mentioned are encouraged to apply for the vacant position, I am always surprised to hear a few well-qualified people shy away from the opportunity, citing the following statement as an excuse:

"I just don't think I'm ready for the responsibility that comes with a higher position, even if it comes with better pay and greater benefits."

This type of attitude is what I would call the fear of success. Despite being one of the most proficient—and therefore, successful—employees amongst a particular staff, such a person reels at the imagined fear of the challenges that come with a higher position. This fear betrays that the individual under examination lacks of confidence in his own abilities; nothing he has previously accomplished has helped him travel on the trajectory of improvement. Instead, he is satisfied with the drudgery of mediocrity and clouds his potential with self-doubt.

Self-doubt is a dangerous thing because it is often what leads people towards prolonged procrastination. Because its nagging persuasiveness often convinces people to turn down amazing opportunities, it also smothers diversity and keeps a person's scope of life extremely narrow. So, how do we combat it?

Remind yourself that diversity is extremely important to becoming a well-rounded person. Recognize that self-doubt is often founded on illegitimate concerns, such as worry about an imagined future that probably is not as challenging as it seems from a distance. Also, remember that any challenge can be overcome with the strength of the self-will; your greatest asset, at the dawn of any opportunity, is your ability to believe that you can achieve. Once you are armed with that belief, the motivation to learn, grow, and adapt to any surroundings will also be available to you and opportunities will open up to reach for higher heights wherever you look.

Self-centered goals

Finally, I believe that people often get caught up in procrastination because the goals that they have set for themselves are not others-centered enough for the consequences of delaying their completion to affect anyone other than the goal-setter. When the goals that people set involve a level of social responsibility, procrastination becomes a much deadlier enemy.

Have you ever stood in line at a grocery store and there is someone in front of you trying to come up with that extra ninety cents they need to pay the full amount owing for groceries? Do you just let that senior or young mother put back an item or two because she does not have the full amount? Or do you diplomatically say, "Here is a dollar, this happens to the best of us," and relieve them of their embarrassment for having to accept that dollar?

As you flip from channel to channel on your TV and you come across an advertisement that is asking you to sponsor a child for a few dollars per month, are you able to keep watching? If you have done your part by sponsoring a child, you would probably be able to keep your TV tuned to that channel. For you, the advertisement would remind you of the work that your few dollars is doing in another part of the world. I encourage you not to let your past hesitation cause you to procrastinate further. Instead, allow a deep compassion to grow within you for those who are in need and use those feelings to motivate you to take action immediately.

Some people claim that they do not want to assist others because the money they give is not reaching the children who need it. While this may sometimes ring true, if you have done your part, that is the best that you can do. If an organization takes some of the money for their administration costs, it is still possible that the child will get at least half of what you have offered and, if we choose to be optimistic about it, we can rejoice in the fact that half a loaf is better than none.

Opportunities for kindness such as these frequently appear in the course of our everyday lives, yet people often hesitate to take action when they arise. They postpone their assistance with the rationalization that they will do it next time, but when next time rolls around, the promise they made to themselves has already left their memory. More than anything, I think that it is this kind of procrastination—sitting on our couches and turning a blind eye, that needs to be taken most seriously and amended the most hastily. After all, it takes very little to change the bad habit of putting off giving help to other people, and, more often than not, a small change can make a big difference. One kind action can create many.

Organization

In order to translate the #1 identity that resides within you into actions that others can see, you need to develop the skill of organization. An organized person has an exponentially higher chance of being successful because his habit of setting and accomplishing goals keeps him from procrastinating. Moreover, an organized person's daily routine of breaking down the day's responsibilities into a task list and completing each task within a specified amount of time is good practice for the steps they need to take in order to achieve their life's ultimate goals, whatever they may be.

Organization is fueled by your self-will. It involves fulfilling your promises to do something when you say you will, whether those promises were made simply to yourself or to someone else. Therefore, by being organized, you also practice authenticity and integrity. Keeping your life in order helps you to become someone who people can trust and depend on.

Now you might be saying, "I know I should be organized, but I can't help sometimes forgetting the things I have to do until it's too late. What can I do?"

The following organizational techniques can help you avoid falling into the trap of "forgetting" important tasks, and thus increase your chances of being responsible, dependable, and successful at achieving the overarching goals you have set for yourself.

The first step to getting organized is making sure you begin your day by writing out a list of tasks you need to complete for that day. In a notebook or daily planner, list out every phone call you have to make, errand you have to run, chore you have to complete, etc. Don't leave out items because you think they seem small or unimportant. It is more likely that you will forget to do something if you do not write it down.

In your daily task list, it is also good to break down bigger tasks like "plan Pete's birthday party" into smaller sub-tasks—such as "call the bakery" and "buy materials for loot bags"—so that you have a better idea of the amount of time it will take you to complete the overarching task. As an added incentive, breaking down bigger tasks into sub-tasks will give you a greater sense of accomplishment when you check items off your list because you will be able to do so more often.

As you go through your day, constantly refer back to your list and check off tasks that have been completed. In order to do this, the notebook or planner you use must be portable and readily accessible. For this reason, some people may choose to use their PDAs or mobile phones to stay organized.

When you reach the end of the day, the tasks that are left outstanding for that day should then be the first items on your list for the next day. By making a task list and referring to it to guide your daily routine, you will find that you can have a better handle on the things that you need to accomplish and you will be a lot less likely to forget both very significant and less significant duties.

Unfortunately, many people who are in the habit of making a task list are still disorganized. The reason for this kind of disorganization is not a lack of awareness about personal responsibilities, but a poor sense of time management. True organization involves knowing what you have to do, knowing how long it will take you to get it done, and successfully prioritizing your life so that you can accomplish your goals in the amount of time you allotted for yourself to complete them. An organized person never rushes because he has pre-assessed his tasks and his available time and arranged his day so that each goal he has set is attainable.

Now you might be saying, "I think you're onto something. I already am in the habit of making a task list, but I still find myself rushing through things—especially in the morning or at the end of the work day. Why is that?"

Most people rush in the mornings or at the end of a work day because of a lack of preparation. Imagine with me what a morning in your household would be like if you decided to 1) get your outfit for work ready the night before, 2) pack your trunk with every item you need to bring to work the next day before you go to sleep, and 3) prepare and bag your lunch after dinner so you won't have to do it in the morning? Why, you might have time in the morning to actually enjoy your cup of coffee instead of grabbing it on-the-go! More importantly, preparing for the day ahead beforehand will leave you time to deal with any emergencies that arise before you leave for work, thus ensuring that even the worst morning catastrophe won't have the opportunity to leave you frazzled.

Another example of a situation where rushing could be avoided by the simple act of preparation is the day before you are scheduled to leave for vacation. Taking a vacation should be a relaxing and enjoyable experience, but, unfortunately, many people's vacations are tarnished by stress and worry because they weren't prepared. When taking a vacation, do not wait until minutes before you leave for the airport to pack. Your packing should start a week before you leave; this will allow you—especially ladies—to make sure you have the correct pairs of earrings or the correct matching top to go with your matching pants. You do not want to get to the beach or to the fancy dinner you have planned for yourself and be disappointed by the realization that you are missing the right hat or the right pair of earrings to go with your other accessories. Also, if possible, it would be helpful to get some currency exchanged ahead of time so that you will have some local currency with you when you travel. Doing this can help you to avoid problems with foreign bank machines and it will save you the panic of not being able to obtain emergency cash when you need it. Having packed your bag, printed your flight schedule, and prepared your foreign currency beforehand, you will not need to rush on the day you are scheduled to leave and can enjoy every minute of the vacation you worked hard to earn and plan for.

Another benefit of not being rushed is that you will, more often than not, show up to appointments both refreshed and on time. Remember, a person who is rushing always looks rushed. By managing your personal time wisely, you will be able to bless others by being punctual for appointments and ready to immediately engage with them at the very moment they arrive. Many people in today's society undervalue the habit of punctuality. However, being on time for appointments and events communicates a great deal about you as a person and being chronically late leaves people with a very bad impression of your work habits and organization skills.

Even if you are only meeting friends and family for an outing, try to be on time. There is nothing worse than having a friend show up at 6:00 p.m. for an appointment that was scheduled for 5:15 p.m. Lateness communicates a lack of respect for the other person's time and the other person's company. If you frequently encounter unforeseen circumstances while travelling between destinations, allot yourself an extra half hour for travelling so you can avoid being late because of traffic or accidents. If you do end up arriving early, the extra time you have is not wasted; you can use it to enjoy the scenery around you, freshen up your make-up, or even relax with a coffee before an engagement. By being early, you will also ensure you are on time and thus will maintain your priceless reputation as an organized person in the eyes of the person you will be meeting.

If you do, however, plan an occasion with someone and something unpreventable causes you to be delayed, pay the person you are meeting with the common courtesy of giving them a phone call to inform them of your tardiness. Even if it might take a bit of effort to get in contact with the person you are meeting with in the case of an emergency, you can show them respect and alleviate any concern they may have for your safety when you notify them of the reason for your absence.

Planning your life well through the use of organizational techniques will not only help you improve your ability to enjoy both your work and play more because you won't have to rush, it will also help you to gain and maintain the trust of the people around you who may greatly benefit you on your road to success. As a final thought, consider the following "organizational buzz-words" and reflect on how they could be better integrated into your life to ensure success:

Results Orientation: Results orientation is the personal drive to pursue the highest possible standards by making the use of all the resources available to you. An organized person will be able to make the most efficient use of every means he can find because he will know how to manage them in a way that will produce the best results.

Initiative: Initiative is the power or ability to begin and to follow through energetically. By staying organized, a person can motivate himself to begin an activity because the steps will be clearly laid out beforehand and he will be certain of what he needs to achieve.

Time—and Self-Management: Time-management involves being able to correctly assess the time you have available to you and prioritize so that you can maximize the amount of work you get done within a limited amount of time. Self-management involves achieving a balance in your work and life between quality times of rest and relaxation and times where you diligently work at your jobs and responsibilities. An organized person possesses excellent time management skills, and thus can optimize his work time so that he can maximize his free time.

Thoroughness: To be thorough means that you comb through every situation or product to make sure there are no errors and that you do an excellent and complete job of completing any task. Organization will help you be thorough because it will instill in you a desire for perfection. Once you have developed the habit of being organized, your heightened awareness of things that are missing or incomplete will help you to rectify any mistakes in whatever work or task that you engage in.

Consider how many of these qualities you currently possess and find ways to improve or incorporate the qualities which you currently lack into your every day life. As an added incentive, remember that an organized person is someone who is always "on top of things" which, in other words, means they are always #1!

Developing a Good Vocabulary

We have already established that, no matter what the world thinks, you were born #1. However, while it should not be essential to your self-image that people recognize you for the winner that you are, it is helpful for you and beneficial for those around you when you are able to radiate your first-place personality to whoever may cross your path.

In this book, I provide advice on how to feel, look, and act like the #1 person that you are. In this chapter, I will introduce another way you can make sure you shine wherever you go: by paying careful attention to how you use your words.

A good vocabulary can help you in your quest to share your first-place personality with others because it makes communicating with others easy. Before you panic and protest that polysyllabic words make you choke, let me assure you that an educated vocabulary does not mean using a slew of unfamiliar words in conversation. Instead, it means you understand how to use words properly to convey your thoughts and ideas with ease.

You don't have to know a lot of unfamiliar words to impress the people you are with. In fact, spitting out a series of polysyllabic words you found in an academic journal might alienate the majority of people you interact with on a daily basis. Instead, a well-spoken person is someone who knows how to use the words he knows effectively and appropriately.

In this chapter, I want to provide you with a few tricks you can use to sharpen your vocabulary and ensure it is in tip-top shape for any conversational or communication opportunity you may encounter.

In today's society, people often do not make it a habit to read for leisure. This is unfortunate, because reading is a primary way through which we acquire new vocabulary. Before you cringe and complain about how books are boring, consider how the practice of reading has changed since we have moved into the Information Age. Informational texts no longer exist solely in the form of books. Many websites, blogs, and online periodicals now provide interesting and well-written content for people who prefer to read in short bursts on an electronic device. The best thing about reading online content is that web writers often condense information into manageable chunks—without forsaking the high-quality diction that will help you maintain a good vocabulary.

Another benefit to reading web content is that it allows you to practice associative thinking as you jump from article to article. This type of non-linear thinking engages the imagination and intuition in making connections and is very valuable in contemporary work environments. Books are written in a more linear structure and, while they are still invaluable to developing a good vocabulary, supplementing them with online content—which you can conveniently access from a mobile device if you happen to have five minutes to spare and want to read—is a good way of staying both informed and current.

Of course, the trick to effective online reading is finding legitimate content. Not all web content is quality content. Gossip magazines, personal blogs, and hobby-specific sites—such as cooking or do-it-yourself instructional sites, are not good sources of online reading. Instead, search for online versions of newsy periodicals such as Maclean's or TIME Magazine, or make a habit of reading the newspaper online. Good web content normally consists of a large block of writing and is written in a formal, rather than informal, tone.

Once you have chosen something to read, it is important that you implement the correct reading strategies to help you make the most of the time you spend reading. When looking to improve your vocabulary through reading, in particular, it is crucial that you resist the bad habit of glossing over words you don't know. Instead, use the following techniques to make those unfamiliar words a permanent part of your vocabulary.

First, when you encounter a new word, underline it or mark it in some way. Then, before you look in a dictionary, try and guess the meaning of the word by using the context clues surrounding the word to create a definition. After you have done that, consult a dictionary to find out the correct definition of the word. (With the accessibility that Google offers, there is no good excuse for not wanting to use a dictionary!) Finally, copy the word and definition down on a piece of paper or a cue card so that you can review it later. Keeping and periodically reviewing a list of new words you are learning will give you a chance to use them more readily in conversation. Furthermore, studies show that if you use a new word three times shortly after learning it, it will establish itself as part of your everyday word bank.

If reading is not something that appeals to you or if you don't have enough time in your day to schedule in even fifteen minutes to read an article online, there are other ways you can increase your mastery of words. The internet now offers a number of different websites that have been created solely for the purpose of helping people learn new words. Applications such as Free Rice, Word Stash, and East of the Web's Define Time are all easily accessible online word games that can be played as a five-minute break from work. The benefit of these word games are two-fold: not only do they help you to acquire new words for your personal vocabulary, they also provide a fun break activity that can stimulate your brain and re-energize it for another long stretch of work.

Of course, the roots of a good vocabulary are best developed when a person is young. Therefore, for parents of young children, it is essential that you develop in your children a love for literacy at a young age. There are many ways you can encourage your child to read. Reading stories with them at bedtime—or during other times in the day—is a good way of modeling reading practices for your kids and engaging them in an activity where they can show you their personal progress over time. Taking weekly trips to the library to pick out books and talk about what makes a good book is also a good way of involving children in the practice of investigating written texts and choosing texts that are both interesting and of high quality. If you feel a little bit clueless about how to choose good books, libraries are stocked full of resources—both print and in-person resources—that can help you to distinguish quality texts from mediocre ones. Taking part in library events with your children and talking to your local librarians are also great ways to develop your knowledge about how to help your children develop their literacy skills.

A final trick to acquiring a good vocabulary comes in the form of a tool that teachers and parents often use to help young people study. This tool is called a *mnemonic device*. Mnemonic devices are patterns of association that we use to help us commit something to memory. For example, my mother's name was Emily and she was a well-respected lady within the community. Therefore, when I was first introduced to the word "eminent" at the age of 7, I associated that word with my mother because her name began with "em" and she was well-known and respected within our community.

You can create your own mnemonic devices by associating unfamiliar words with familiar ideas that bear a resemblance to the word itself. The beauty of mnemonic devices is that they will help you create a personal connection with words that ultimately enriches your vocabulary when you put it to use.

Personal Moments

In the busyness of today's world, it can be easy to forget that you were indeed born #1. The adversity you face every day can drain you of the willpower you need to succeed, and hurt and disappointment can cause your compassion for others to wane. Thus, taking the time to rest, relax, and celebrate what it is that makes you 'you' is an essential part of maintaining your well-being.

In the following pages, I provide a few suggestions of activities and environments that can inspire in you the positive feelings of comfort, tranquillity, and pleasure that your day-to-day responsibilities can often deprive you of. As you consider each image, notice that the people depicted are unafraid to pamper themselves. The ability to give yourself special attention on occasion is a way you can re-affirm for yourself that you are truly #1.

1) Personal moments can be simple. You do not need to go somewhere special or spend a lot of money to enjoy a personal moment. Set aside an evening to relax beside the fireplace (or somewhere equally as cozy) with a glass of wine. As you sit, allow yourself to fully relish the comfort and warmth of your home. Reflect on the things you have achieved and quietly affirm yourself as you delight in your moment of rest.

2) Personal moments can be practical. When you do not have enough time in your schedule to add any special activities, learn to turn your everyday activities into personal moments. Adding a few bath salts or bubbles to your bath and lighting a few candles can make an everyday chore become a time of relaxation. Don't let busyness steal your ability to enjoy yourself. Make everyday moments a source of delight by using your creativity!

3) Personal moments can involve treasured possessions. Do you have a special teacup-and-saucer set that you save only for important occasions or crystal glasses you break out only during the fanciest of dinner parties? Make a day special by treating yourself to the use of these beautiful things. Treat yourself as a guest of honour by sitting down for a quiet moment with your "for-company-only silverware" and let yourself delight in the visual or tactile exquisiteness that made you value these possessions in the first place.

4) Personal moments can take place at any time during the day. More often than not, people take personal moments in the late afternoon or in the evening, after the stress of the day has taken its toll. While this has its benefits, making the habit of carving out the time for personal moments in the mornings can also go a long way in improving your outlook on the rest of your day. Turn your kitchen into a place where you want to spend mornings by adding a comfortable breakfast area or buying that espresso machine you always wanted. You may find your dreaded morning routine turns into a time to celebrate the day when you take care to treat it as such.

5) Personal moments involve your senses. In an idea-driven society, we often spend too much time in our heads and not enough time appreciating our bodies. Take a hint from the more European habit of occasionally indulging your senses. Treat yourself to a delicious snack and a good glass of wine. Put on your favourite music and give yourself time to just sit and listen to it. Snuggle up with your favourite blanket and feel its delicious fuzziness. Pleasuring your senses will cause your body to relax and will give your mind a break from the stressors that keep you tense throughout the day.

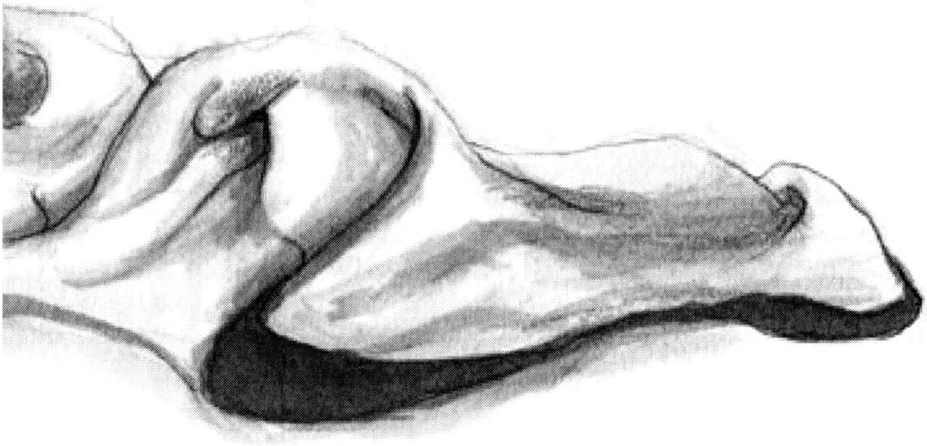

6) Personal moments can include others. Spending quality time with a close family member or friend can do wonders for your self-esteem. The encouragement and affirmation you receive from a conversation with someone who truly cares about you can help remind you of the qualities that make you #1 when you are in danger of forgetting them. However, quality time with another person does not always have to include words. Sharing an activity or simply being in the presence of a loved one can give you the comfort and reassurance you need to learn to love yourself.

7) Personal moments do not always have to happen while you are awake. Sleep has become somewhat of a functional commodity in our world. People never seem to get enough of it, nor do they make the time they spend sleeping special and sacred. If you are not in the habit of making your bedroom a sanctuary for rest, find a place that specializes in helping you create a relaxing environment—like a spa or a resort, and book yourself an appointment to give yourself time for intentional rest. Otherwise, outfitting your bedroom with aromatherapy candles and comfortable sheets and moving your workspace or home office into another room can help to make your bedroom a place where sleep becomes a sensual delight.

8) Personal moments can take place outdoors. Technology has begun to usurp the amount of time people spend outdoors soaking in the sun and breathing fresh air, which is unfortunate because simply being in nature can rejuvenate your body and soul in ways that doing anything else indoors cannot. If you are the type of person who spends most of your time with your eyes glued to a television or computer screen, book some time off to take a stroll in one of the many beautiful parks your city has to offer. If there isn't a park near you, take a walk through your neighbourhood instead. Soak in the smell of the freshly cut grass on people's lawns or newly pruned rosebushes in your neighbour's garden. Listen carefully to the rustling of the trees in the wind. Soak in the warmth of the sun and feel the sponginess of fresh dirt under the soles of your shoes. As you walk, remind yourself that you are intimately connected with the natural world around you simply by the matter you are made up of. Allow the natural world to remind you what it feels like to be truly alive.

9) Personal moments may involve physical activity. For men, in particular, personal moments often involve some sort of work. Whether it is tinkering with the underside of a car in the garage or lifting weights at a gym, a personal moment for you may mean doing something rewarding that makes you sweat. The beauty of such active personal moments is that you become very aware of the many parts of your body working together to accomplish a personal goal. Allow yourself to relish in the satisfaction of reaching a new personal best or completing a project that you have always dreamed of finishing.

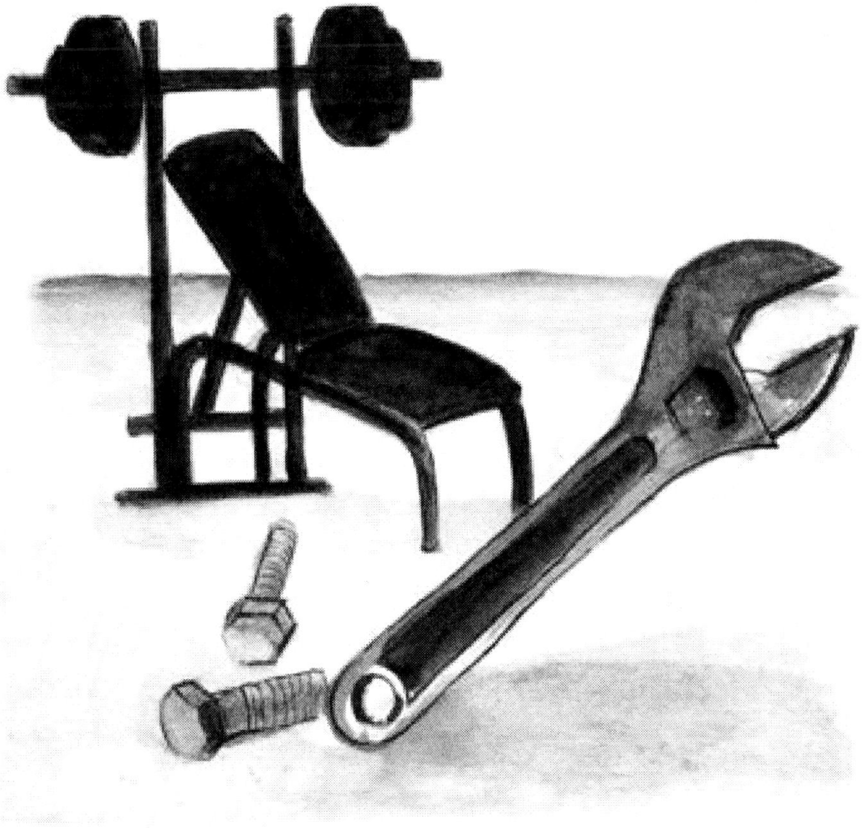

10) Personal moments can be culturally enriching. Activities like listening to jazz music or spending time in a museum can inspire in you the serenity you seek in a personal moment, while simultaneously expanding your knowledge of the world. When taking part in cultural hobbies, allow your mind and heart to wander and don't neglect how you feel in favour of sharpening your intellect. Rather, allow both head and heart to work in harmony as you let the art or music you are partaking of teach you more about the nuances of life.

These examples are just starting points to help you consider the kinds of activities and environments you may want to adopt or identify as personal moments for yourself. The key to creating downtime that produces real rest and rejuvenation is making that time special and personal to you.

If planning purposeful downtime is a new concept for you, I suggest that you do the following. Set aside a time to create a list of activities and environments which make you feel the most at peace with yourself and the world. Don't allow yourself to feel frivolous or unproductive for wanting to spend time simply doing something you enjoy. Include the most seemingly insignificant things if they are what make you feel special.

After you have done that, take a look at your schedule and allot times in the following weeks or months that you can set aside to engage in these activities. Remember, a personal moment doesn't have to take long; something as simple as taking fifteen minutes at the end of a difficult week to treat yourself to ice-cream or listening to encouraging music on your way to work can be considered a personal moment as long as it celebrates you, so be liberal with the number of personal moments you allow yourself to have! (More often than not, people take much less time for themselves than they need or deserve.)

Finally, remember that an essential part of feeling like you are #1 is treating yourself like you are #1. Creating and enjoying personal moments will help you to re-affirm the qualities that make you a unique individual and it will go a long way in reminding you of your self-worth.

Positives and Negatives

Your reaction to any problem you might encounter can be monitored on a spectrum bookended by two extremes; on one end of the spectrum is the positive outlook, that helps you to see everything through rose-coloured glasses, and on the other end of the spectrum is the negative outlook, the feeling that naturally overcomes a person when he is faced with adversity. The key to feeling like a #1 individual, no matter what situation you find yourself in, is found in learning to find a healthy balance between these two extremes, with your primary instinct always leaning slightly more towards the positive end of the spectrum.

The reason why a lot of people tend to feel down about difficult or uncertain situations is because they have unconsciously adopted an attitude of *protective pessimism* towards life. Protective pessimism is a coping mechanism that people develop, often after experiencing unfulfilled hopes, to avoid being disappointed when life doesn't go their way. Although it sounds like a negative behaviour, protective pessimism isn't necessarily a bad thing. There are some situations in life when we have to be realistic about what we should allow ourselves to hope for.

For example, if a relative that you know has been suffering for a long time from a terminal illness and the doctor has just sent him to palliative care because his condition is critical, protective pessimism might help you to prepare for the chances that he may not survive this relapse. This type of preparation can help you to be more intentional about making his last days comfortable and valuable to both him and those around you.

The point at which protective pessimism becomes dangerous occurs when a person refuses to see anything through the lens of hope, for fear that any kind of positive wish he may have will lead to disappointment. This kind of protective pessimism often expresses itself in anger, bitterness, irritability, and, in more extreme cases, morbidity and despair. In these cases, protective pessimism needs to be checked by its more positive counterpart: *prudent optimism.*

More often than not, when we hear the word optimism, the first thing that comes into our minds is the well-meaning, but empty encouragement people dole out to a person who comes face to face with adversity.

"Just believe that everything will be okay."

"Don't worry, something better will come along soon."

This brand of optimism, though popular, is inherently empty of power because 1) it ignores reality and 2) it is based on the belief that a person undergoing a trial is a victim of his own circumstances. The idea that a bad situation will miraculously disappear on its own is an illusion; a bad situation only gets better when a person willfully makes it better by making choices that can help him overcome the present obstacle and create a better future for himself.

Instead of prompting you to gloss over the harsh realities that can accompany a difficult time in life, prudent optimism involves gauging your circumstances with a critical eye and making a willful decision to see the realistic opportunities that are available to you amidst the hardship. Let us go back to the example of the company downsizing that I mentioned in an earlier chapter.

In this type of scenario, a person who practices empty optimism may be able to stay positive for a few weeks after his job loss by telling himself that "something better will come along." He may casually begin a job search, repressing his worry by living in the illusion that the perfect job he is looking for is somewhere out there, lined up for him to take. However, as the months roll on and he encounters rejection after rejection, his positive energy will begin to falter. His false belief that circumstances can change without his willful input has led him to take a wishy-washy approach to making the best of his future. Instead of taking note of the realities of a recession economy or, perhaps, realizing his own need to update his skills to match a changing market, he stubbornly hangs onto the hope that a good thing will come along if he just believes hard enough in his own positive outlook. Unfortunately, this kind of false hope is not enough to sustain the growing disappointment that he encounters and he eventually falls victim to bitterness and anger towards his personal situation.

On the other hand, a person who practices prudent optimism would refrain from making a blanket statement about his feelings towards his lay off. This person realizes that, in a recession economy, a job may not be easy to find. Because of this, he makes plans to improve and add to his available skills by taking additional courses or earning another professional degree. He considers the kinds of opportunities for personal growth that he can make a priority as a result of this lay off, which can also replace the sense of worth he received from having a job—spending more time investing in his children or taking the steps to make a side career out of his hobbies, for example. By making these types of decisions, this prudent optimist gives himself concrete reasons to have a positive outlook. Although he may not be completely certain that every new goal he has set will be met with success, he has much more of a reason to hope in their fulfillment because he has carefully considered their attainability beforehand.

Now you might be saying, "That sounds great, but how do I practice prudent optimism in my own life?"

The key to unlocking the door to prudent optimism in your life is learning to see circumstances from a new point of view. Instead of seeing an event in your life as inherently positive or negative, learn to see it as neutral. Convince yourself that the positive and negative connotations each event seems to have is a result of your own perspective on it, and you will soon begin to see that you are in the position of power to change your perspective on a situation.

The fact is that anyone can have a positive outlook on life if he really wants to because staying positive is essentially an act of the will. Any kind of optimism requires you to resolutely believe in a better tomorrow. The benefit of prudent optimism is that it provides concrete reasons—in the form of attainable goals—that can help you sustain that belief when circumstances seemingly fail to improve.

As an example of what I mean when I say that events in life should be seen as neutral is provided below in the form of a chart. In the left column are examples of situations that are often perceived as having a negative connotation to them. In the middle and right columns, I have provided two opposing ways of looking at the same event: positive and negative.

Event	Positive Outlook	Negative Outlook
Job loss	– More time to refresh and update skills – More time to spend with family – Opportunity to change careers – Opportunity to meet new people and have new experiences – Job loss is a result of a larger set of circumstances, not a personal failure	– Trapped in a rut of financial instability – Lack of purpose because there is no job title to help secure your identity – Job loss is a communication of a personal failure
Health crisis	– A chance to rest and recover from the everyday cycle of stress and burn-out – The opportunity to grow close to friends and family and treasure the gift of life – The chance to sympathize with others suffering from similar difficulties and be a blessing in their lives	– A financial burden because you have to take time off work – Embarrassment because you can no longer be self-sufficient – Health crisis is the result of some kind of universal force that wants to punish you or spite you with suffering

As you can see, the exact same event can be approached in two very different ways. When a person chooses to look at it through the lens of prudent optimism, any event—however difficult, can produce a multitude of blessing in his life. However, when a person chooses to look at it through the lens of unchecked pessimism, negativity saps any potential the person has of overcoming the obstacle.

Choose to maintain an attitude of prudent optimism by remembering the following characteristics about positive and negative outlooks, and make it a habit to adopt the first set of qualities while avoiding the second:

Positive	**Negative**
Has internal motivation	Lacks internal motivation
Stays organized	Nothing about their lives is organized
Tries to set goals and achieve them	Does not set any goals and therefore achieves nothing
Looks for the best in every situation	Looks for the worst in every situation
Looks at a glass as always half full	Looks at a glass as always half empty

Heroes

Every hero's life began as a collision between a spermatozoa and an egg in the belly of a young woman who has been granted the honour of being a mother. The essential circumstances of a hero's birth—which are marvellously special—are no different than the circumstances of any person's birth, which means that every person that has ever been born—you included—was destined to be a hero.

"But," you might say to me, "aren't heroes strong and mighty? Don't they perform extraordinary acts? I sure don't feel like I was destined to be a hero. I feel small and timid, and I haven't done anything extraordinary in my lifetime."

I want to debunk the common misconception that being a hero means you have to be Superman. In fact, what qualifies you to be a hero is not any type of superhuman ability, but rather a profound love of mankind that motivates you to offer all of your life and efforts to serve the rest of humanity. While it is nearly impossible to develop superhuman capabilities, compassion for others can grow with time and serving others can become a habit through practice.

As I have mentioned throughout this book, the most powerful tool a person has in the quest for self-improvement is willpower. Therefore, the first step to reclaiming the sense of heroism you were gifted with at birth is seeing yourself as the hero you are meant to be. By choosing to subscribe to the identity you have been destined for, you are readying yourself for victory by envisioning the end goal. (Olympic athletes often use this technique while training to motivate themselves toward success.) Remind yourself daily to be a hero because you were born to be one. Say to yourself, "I am a hero because I want to be one, I choose to be one, and I was born to be one. I am a hero because I am willing to do whatever it takes to give everything I have to serve others."

After completing that first step of acknowledging that you were born to be a hero, it is time to begin taking ownership of that identity by practicing heroic deeds in your life.

"But," you might say, "I have no idea what heroic deeds look like. How, then, can I go about performing them?"

Just as a young child learns to be a man or a woman by imitating the actions of the adults around them, you can learn to be a hero by mimicking the actions of heroes you know.

Finding real heroes to learn from can be difficult because of the type of glamourized heroism that has been incorrectly advertised by the media. The publicized heroes of our day and age—celebrities, politicians, men and women who have vaults upon vaults of money to spare—are often unfairly crowned for their simplistic and, all-too-often, rare acts of kindness because of their proximity to sources of media. Unfortunately, the lives that these so-called "heroes" lead do not always reflect the true heroism that is worth imitation.

To counteract this faulty understanding of heroism, I would like to offer an opposing point-of-view. I believe that true heroes are often found in the most unglamourous of places, sharing life with people who society has deemed the most unglamourous of all. They are rarely seen or heard by the general public because they spend most of their time and energy loving those who society has rejected and helping outcasts feel like the #1 people they were born to be. True heroes are not always rich nor are they interested in being lauded for their achievements; they simply are those who see whatever they have been given—money, status, talents, or otherwise—as a way to bless others and act accordingly. They are heroes because they have decided for themselves that the world could use a hero and thus, they have given their lives to fill that position.

When you take the time to think about it, you will find that true heroes are all around you. In fact, the first place you should look for them is in your own neighbourhood. The people who have had the greatest positive impact in your life will almost always be examples of what a true hero is like. The teacher who spoke a kind word to you when no one else would pay you any attention, the parent who took days off work to make soup for you or to take you to the doctor when you got sick, the senior in your neighbourhood who devoted their hard-earned retirement years to serving the community in a multitude of ways—these are all examples of heroes you should seek to emulate.

In my own life, I have a sister who I consider to be an example of an everyday hero. My sister inspires me to be heroic because of the way she uses her gifts and talents to bless those around her. Every week, my sister will devote one entire day to baking—her favourite hobby. On that day, she will prepare an assortment of bread and cookies and wrap them up in little baggies, so that she can, throughout the week, distribute them to a tired pastor, a lonely neighbour, or a sickly patient as a way of cheering them up. Her diligence in keeping up this regular routine and her willingness to spend her own pocket money to bless those in need makes her one of my personal heroes.

After you have found an example or two of a true hero in your everyday life, the next step is to observe them and develop a closer relationship with them. I have often found that conversing with the heroes who inspire me to action often leads me to more examples of everyday heroes and gives me the opportunity to absorb the compassion that radiates from heroic hearts. It may sound far-fetched in theory, but being around a compassionate person and witnessing the moments in which they choose to perform a kind action will unlock within you the innate compassion you were born with. Kindness in one person can activate the kindness of many.

In the following pages, I would like to share with you a few stories of everyday heroes who I have had the blessing of hearing about and who I hope will inspire you to search for and become a hero in your own right.

I was watching CNN one day they were airing a story about how an ordinary manicurist named Lidia Schaefer embraced her calling to do extraordinary things with the average life she was given. Before she fully realized her identity as a hero, Lidia Schaefer was just a regular nail expert who served the men and women in her local neighbourhood by providing nail care services. Yet, despite being raised to believe that she could achieve the cushy life she had always dreamed of having if she just worked hard, she found herself dissatisfied; she felt that she could do more to help the world than working a day job and earning money to fund her personal interests. So, she traded in the trappings of her American dream, selling her house and car to help build a school in her native village in Ethiopia. Today, her school serves nearly 1,500 students per day and provides local children with the chance for a better life by means of a proper education. For Lidia, it was a matter of doing what she felt was right and not listening to the many people around her that warned her about the dangers of working with her heart and not her head.

Roy Foster is another man who was featured on CNN for his testimony of how he turned his very ordinary life—marred for a time by a crippling addiction—into a heroic life by choosing to love and serve others with his experiences. Roy Foster was an ex-alcoholic Army Veteran when he started Stand Down House to help Veterans who were struggling with addiction and homelessness in Florida. Since 2000, his program has provided life-changing services to nearly 900 Veterans. He finds homeless Vets in vacant lots behind supermarkets or small clearings off the highway and takes them in for counselling, rehabilitation services, and personal care. Foster works with his local sheriff's homeless outreach units to find Veterans who often live in tents or makeshift lean-tos because they cannot afford better housing, and personally delivers to them a message that there is help for them if they need it. His own experience as an alcoholic provides him with the compassion and motivation to reach out to the men he works with on a daily basis and the story of his recovery is an encouragement to all those he encounters who may believe that they are beyond help.

I would encourage you to follow the examples of Lidia and Roy. Consider what material things, time, experiences, skills and talents you have to offer and commit to changing the way you view your personal belongings. Imagine the amount of good you could do if you dedicated everything you had to the service of others and find small ways to begin implementing that mentality in your daily interactions with people.

Find a couple in your community who would be blessed by a night away from the kids and offer to host a play-date at your house so that the parents can go on a date. Seek out a family who could use a good home-cooked meal every once in a while because they don't have time to prepare their own and whip up your favourite homestyle recipe for them. Send a letter to someone you know is having a hard time and include words of encouragement to help them through their day.

Be creative! There are so many ways you can offer your unique skills to serve others, ranging from small acts of kindness to incredible feats of self-denial (which you can work up to if you persist in learning to become more others-centred.) Just remember that the choice you make to give your life up for the benefit of others is the choice to be a hero. You never know—your act of kindness might end up saving someone's day!

Parenting

Parenting can be one of the most rewarding responsibilities a person takes on in his or her lifetime. The wonder of bringing a child into the world, the joy of watching him grow up, and the comfort of having grown children love and care for you when you get older are just some of the many benefits of being a parent. However, many people do not realize that the title "parent" is not a circumstantial label we can carelessly slap onto any person who has experienced the miracle of childbirth. The act of becoming a parent requires self-will; it is a choice to live a life of sacrificial love in order to provide a child with everything he needs to grow up feeling like the #1 person he was born to be.

Consider with me the following scenario. During a passionate night of love-making, a young couple conceives a child. Because the pregnancy was unplanned, it takes both the man and the woman by surprise. Nevertheless, the couple decide to go through with having the child, and, nine months later, the child is born into their home. In this type of situation, the expecting couple has to make a choice about how they will handle this unexpected addition to their family.

On one hand, they may treat it like a mistake—a physical consequence of not having been more careful. This kind of attitude causes the couple to care for the child out of obligation or duty—because they are aware that he has certain undeniable physical needs. Though they might spend money on feeding, clothing, and housing him, their hearts ultimately remain devoted to their personal comfort and independence. Therefore, in circumstances where their child's needs are not critical and the couple has the luxury of choosing their own needs over those of their child—choosing to watch the primetime television show that airs every night around his bedtime instead of tucking him into bed, for instance—nine times out of ten, this couple will give into their own desires. Because they never let the child change their ideas of what brings them joy, he is left wondering if he has inconvenienced his parents from living the lives they truly desire.

On the other hand, the young couple could see the unexpected pregnancy as a miracle. In this case, though the pregnancy was unplanned, the couple makes the effort to re-organize their lives so that they can give their child the best life they can offer him. Deep down, this couple knows that the decision to put their child's needs above their own will result in some painful sacrifices. Yet, despite the inconvenience he has caused for them, they choose to see him as a treasured possession. Bettering his life now becomes their number one goal, and, as he grows up, they take every opportunity they can to serve him in both essential and non-essential ways. The child of this couple is aware that, no matter what, his parents will always be there for him, no matter what his concerns are. He doesn't feel guilty for asking them to nourish him or nurture him because deep down he knows that their love for him enables them to enjoy performing even the most inconvenient of tasks.

Now I ask you: which of these two couples would you consider to be true parents? Is it the couple who begrudgingly feeds their child because they have to live with the consequences of their mistake? Or is it the couple who makes a commitment to learn to treat their child as their beloved one, sacrificing for him even their most precious desires and belongings?

I am sure you would agree that the couple who chose the path of sacrificial love are the true parents.

"Wow," you might say to me, "I never realized, but I think I'm more like the first couple than the second one. Is it too late for me to change now that I have already seen my child through a good number of years?"

Definitely not! It is never too late to begin improving your relationship with your child. If you haven't made the commitment to sacrificially love your child no matter what the cost, today is the day to do it. You *and* your child will benefit from your decision to put him first because being a good parent will help both of you feel like the #1 people you were made to be.

Now you might be thinking, "Alright, I've made that commitment to love my child sacrificially and to put him first in every circumstance. What are some practical things I can do right away to put that love into action?"

The first course of action I would suggest to you would be to find your child and remind him that *he is loved.* If you have not established the routine of saying "I love you," make it a habit that begins today. Find time at least once a day—or more, if you remember—to tell your child how much you love him. Reflect on the qualities in your child that make him special and make those known to him. Empower him with words of encouragement and remind him regularly that he is #1. A parent's love goes a long way in helping a person feel like the first-place individual that he is.

For parents with older children, remember that a child needs to hear the words, "I love you. You are special to me," from the moment they are born until the day they die. In fact, the older your children get, the more powerful their reliance on your love they will be because it is your love that will anchor them during their times of trial.

In addition to making a habit of saying "I love you," make the effort to spend quality time with him. If this means neglecting your Saturday plans to work on your personal hobby so that you can watch your son's baseball game or TiVo-ing your favourite primetime television show so you can tuck your daughter into bed, do it and do it right away. Young children, in particular, desperately need quality time with their parents because it is during those times when they receive the one-on-one attention and affection that children are wired to crave.

For younger children, the half-hour to forty-five minute window right before they go to bed is great for "daddy-and-me" or "mommy-and-me" time. Instead of simply tucking them into their bed and turning off the light, establish a routine where you sit with your child after tucking him in so that the two of you can talk about his day. While your child is talking, make him feel safe by cuddling with him or responding affectionately to what he is saying with empathetic "m-hmms" and nods of understanding. Allow your child the room to share whatever is on his heart, letting him know that you are there to walk with him through whatever problem he is having.

After you have spent some time conversing with your child about the concerns that are on his heart, prepare him for bed by reading him a bedtime story. When my sons were younger, I used to read to them just about every night because I believed that reading to my children would help them grow in their understanding of the world. I also believed that it would eventually contribute to the development of their literacy skills. I remember very well how my sons looked forward to that time we spent together and how much comfort they took from hearing my voice and feeling me ease out of their bed as they drifted to sleep. Reading to my sons had become an honoured tradition in my family that my children look back on and remember fondly.

Parental influence is strongest when children are young. Therefore, the greatest act of love you can perform for your children is to invest every ounce of time and energy you have into spending time with them while they are still developing and impressionable.

When your child is sitting in front of the TV during his free time, sit and have a conversation with him about what he is watching. Be aware of the messages that are filtering into your child's brain and be there to filter out the negative ones before they have a chance to take hold.

Use meal times to teach your children manners. Take up a family hobby that both you and your child can share, such as playing sports or doing arts and crafts. Take weekly trips to the park and to the library and engage your children in developing both their brains and their bodies while they are there.

Take family vacations. People underestimate the power of family time spent away from home because the word "vacation" often implies to them an expensive getaway opportunity that they just cannot afford. The fact is: good vacations don't have to cost a lot of money. A simple weekend getaway to a nearby campground or cottage district can provide your family with ample time to get to know each other and create experiences that your family can reminisce on for years to come.

Ultimately, the best piece of advice I can offer you about spending quality time with your child is this: Don't wait for opportunities to come to you. Make them happen.

As children grow older, both parents and children tend to develop a more laissez-faire attitude towards spending quality time together. All too often, not making family time a priority results in parents and children never spending any time together at all. This is a serious problem because it is during the quality time that you spend with your child when you can teach and remind your child of the core values he will need as he matures into an adult. Oftentimes, the lack of quality time between parents and their teenaged children is what motivates young people to search elsewhere for that same familial bond. Unfortunately, in many cases, that search for belonging leads young people into joining dangerous communities like gangs, cliques, or online forums—all of which open them up to physical, emotional, and sexual predators that can wreak havoc on their reputations and their self-esteem.

If you are a parent of an older child, you may have to use a little creativity in order to find opportunities for quality time with your child that won't make them feel like you are babying him. But, don't let the challenge of re-inventing your parent-and-child traditions scare you into not doing anything at all. Instead, make an extra effort to discover the facets of your child's changing identity, find any point of connection between the two of you, and jump in. Though you may encounter the resistance that normally accompanies teenage rebellion, be persistent and you will find that your child will one day appreciate the effort you put into loving him even when he was not-as-adorable.

All in all, parenting is the process of helping a child grow up believing that he is #1. Without a parent's unconditional love, a child has no model for what it means for someone to treat him like a first-rate individual. He also has no one to protect him from the negative messages society sends him that challenge his sense of self-worth. Choose to be a loving parent to your child today and help restore in the next generation the truth that they are born to be #1.

Authenticity and Integrity

In an earlier chapter, I mentioned that the skill of organization is closely connected with the qualities of authenticity and integrity. However, as we all know, being authentic and having integrity means far more than keeping a neat house and not being late for appointments. Being authentic and having integrity are key characteristics of a #1 individual because they ensure that the way you act lines up with what you say.

Of all the seminars and courses that I have taken in my life time, a week-long, intensive seminar on "Authenticity and Integrity" really stood out to me because it helped me to realize that, although we use those words so commonly in our society, many people take their true meanings far too lightly. Through the seminar, I was encouraged and reminded that the truest test of authenticity and integrity occurs in your reaction to the small things—how we respond to the tedious responsibilities we have to tend to in our everyday lives and how we treat the strangers that we interact with while we are out running errands, for example. To my great surprise, shortly after the seminar, I was able to put my own authenticity and integrity to the test on an outing I took with my family to celebrate the family businesses.

One of the items on the one-week celebration was a walk, in which hundreds of customers took part. The walk took place in a part of the country where there were lots of hills, slopes, and plateaus. It started at 6:00 a.m. and was scheduled to conclude at around 10:00 a.m., with no time to rest scheduled within those four hours for any of the participants. The main objective of the walk was to test each participant's ability to persevere and the goal for each person was to the finish the walk.

Along with all the members of my family, I made a promise before starting that we were going to complete the journey. The journey, for us, represented the highs, lows, slopes, and successes of the two family businesses that were started twenty-five years ago. After the initial stretch of the walk however, the symbolism of the journey began to fade in our minds as we began to get tired. As the families hosting the event, cars were prepared to drive us the rest of the route if we got too tired to continue, and, midway through the journey, the possibility of sitting in a car and enjoying the scenery instead of sweating and walking up and down the hilly landscape was very tempting. However, my sister—who took the seminar on "Authenticity and Integrity" with me—and I remembered what we had learned about being true to our promises, so we led by example and fulfilled our promise to complete that walk. By the simple act of enduring until the end of the walk instead of taking the easy way out, we were able to show our customers that our family is true to our word and reassure them that their trust in us is not in vain.

In addition to developing a strong self-will, being authentic and having integrity make up the foundation of a #1 individual. Practicing both qualities ensures that you are able to walk away from every obstacle with your head held high rather than hung low in shame because authenticity and integrity keep you from engaging in the wrong kind of personal compromise. They are good guards and good advertisers of your unique #1 personality.

In the final pages of this chapter, let us examine other significant personal attributes that go hand in hand with authenticity and integrity. All of these characteristics are also built on the foundation of the self-will and, when developed, will enrich the first-place identity that you have begun to embrace.

Accountability: Being accountable means that people can count on you to 1) complete the task at hand and 2) give them an accurate report of how you have managed whatever you have been given—whether it be time, tasks, people, or money. A person who practices authenticity and integrity accounts for each of these things in every project that he does by making daily lists and reports so that they have an answer for any inquiry that might come their way regarding their stewardship or performance.

Compassion: Being compassionate involves being able to empathize with others in their times of celebration and their times of suffering; it is lived out in the habit of consistently thinking of others before yourself. A person who practices authenticity and integrity is not only concerned about their own personal rights but the rights that every human being is entitled to. This authentic understanding of justice leads them to be compassionate when they see that others are being passed over or oppressed, and their sense of integrity leads them to action on behalf of those in need.

Honesty: Honesty is a commitment to being truthful about both your successes and your shortcomings. A person who practices authenticity and integrity is humble enough to admit when they have failed; they do not hide their shortcomings because they know that lying will only fuel a sense of false respect in others. Instead, they present themselves as they are and gain the trust of others by being candid about their failures and by being genuine in their desire to improve.

Perseverance: Perseverance is a product of the self-will. It is the commitment to keep on going in the face of adversity. A person who practices authenticity and integrity often has to call upon his ability to persevere because choosing to live uprightly means not running backwards when problems come your way. Thankfully, the ability to persevere is built into the core of who you are. If you remember the analogy of a spermatozoa racing towards the egg, you will realize that your ability to persevere has been proved by your own history. You simply have to take that innate ability and empower yourself with it as you leap towards success!

Analogy of Life

1) Your life began as a love story between a man and a woman. In a moment of passion, sperm from the man's body raced towards the egg in the woman's body in a winner-take-all race which resulted in your conception. From that moment on, you were a self-determined individual—dearly loved, uniquely made, and in control of your own destiny.

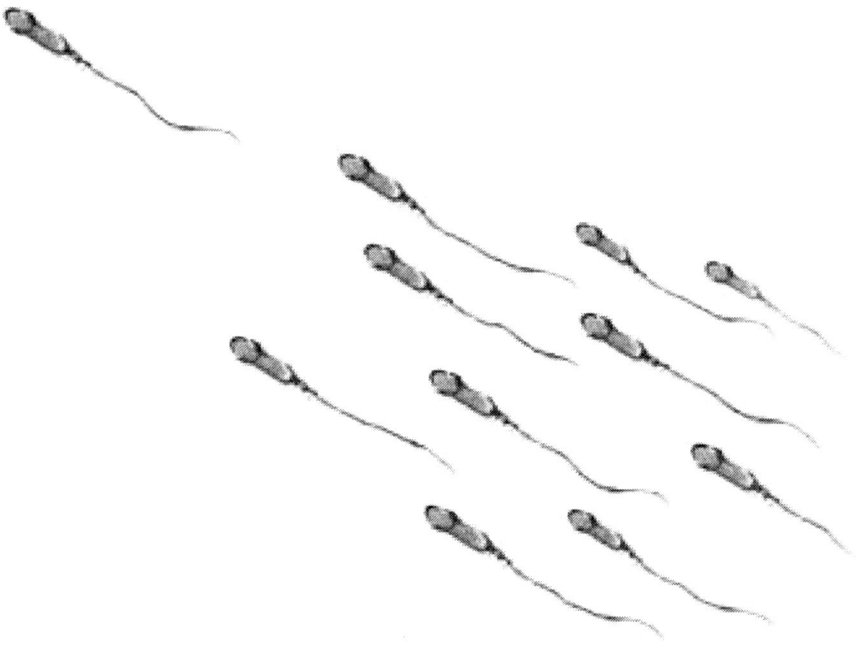

2) As a baby, your mother nurtured you as you fought to survive and yearned to mature both physically and mentally.

3) When you reached childhood, you became consciously aware of love—both in the form of affection and discipline, and you learned to reciprocate it as well. The experiences you had as a child in your home helped to shape your personality, and early instances of adversity strengthened your will power.

4) As you matured into adulthood, love became a more complicated thing; you learned that love involves both a passionate delight and a willful decision. You realized that the people who sweep you off your feet are often the same people who can hurt you most deeply. Your inner strength and your character are shaped by how you choose to love and learn to be loved by these significant individuals.

5) By the time you are middle-aged, your life has become a wealth of personal experience. Your willpower has become strong after overcoming the obstacles you have faced and you are full of joy when you think about the blessings you have received. You realized that the wisdom you have acquired can become a well of refreshment that people can draw from and you gave freely of yourself to your children and to those whom you encounter on a daily basis.

6) In your final days, you were surrounded by the many people you blessed throughout your life—your children, your grand-children, your family and your friends. All gather around you to celebrate the beautiful ending of a life well-lived. In your final moment, your loved ones witness you taking your last breath with a smile because, upon reflection, you are satisfied with the way you have spent your time on earth.

In memory of the days you spent living and as a testament to the legacy you leave behind, your tombstone reads:

A Letter to June

Dear June,

How are things up in heaven? We all miss you very much. Your daughters are strong; you have raised them very well.

Since you departed from this earth on my birthday four years ago, I have shared my birthday roses with you each year, as promised. Since your passing, whenever I take the time to reflect on our years of friendship, sometimes I shed a tear, but most times I find myself smiling from ear to ear, as I attempt to relive our years of reflecting, as we talked and talked for hours over a bottle of wine about our junior years.

We all do appreciate you watching over us. I write not only for myself but I am representing your family and friends acknowledging to you their love, friendship and admiration which was so eloquently reciprocated when you were with us. You will forever be in our hearts.

Love Always,
Cynthia

Acknowledgments

I would like to acknowledge Darren Hogarth, author of the novel *Whatever Sticks Most*, for his critiquing of this manuscript. Thank you for your honest opinion.

I would also like to extend my deepest gratitude to my editor Heidi Lam and illustrator Gigi Wong for all their diligent work on this project. Thank you for so promptly making all changes, adjustments and requests that I asked of you during this process. I am truly blessed to have had your assistance on this project and I took comfort in the fact that you both knew the true person that I am.

LIVE
your life
with the same sense
of fearless passion
that you had when
your life first began.

Deal with
the situation
&
MOVE ON

Making choices in
– FAITH –
that tomorrow
holds the possibility
for better returns
will help you make
wiser choices.

When life gives you
the Lemons
you weren't expecting,
be creative
and make
Lemonade